The Enneagram Test Book

A Practical Guide to Self-Discovery & Self-Realization for Better Relationships and a Better Life: Best Audiobooks & Books; Book 2

Carly Greene

© **Copyright 2020 - All rights reserved.**

The content contained within this book may not be reproduced, duplicated or transmitted without direct written permission from the author or the publisher.

Under no circumstances will any blame or legal responsibility be held against the publisher, or author, for any damages, reparation, or monetary loss due to the information contained within this book, either directly or indirectly.

Legal Notice:

This book is copyright protected. It is only for personal use. You cannot amend, distribute, sell, use, quote or paraphrase any part, or the content within this book, without the consent of the author or publisher.

Disclaimer Notice:

Please note the information contained within this document is for educational and entertainment purposes only. All effort has been executed to present accurate, up to date, reliable, complete information. No warranties of any kind are declared or implied. Readers acknowledge that the author is not engaged in the rendering of legal, financial, medical or professional advice. The content within this book has been derived from various sources. Please consult a licensed professional before attempting any techniques outlined in this book.

By reading this document, the reader agrees that under no circumstances is the author responsible for any losses, direct or indirect, that are incurred as a result of the use of the information contained within this document, including, but not limited to, errors, omissions, or inaccuracies.

Table of Contents

Table of Contents
Introduction
The Questionnaire
Interpreting THE QUEST
Type One: THE REFORMER

    The Childhood Pattern
    Practices Which Help Ones Develop

    Keys for Reflection

Type Two: THE HELPER

    The Childhood Pattern
    Practices Which Help Twos Develop

    Keys for Reflection

Type Three: THE ACHIEVER

    The Childhood Pattern
    Practices Which Help Threes Develop

    Keys for Reflection

Type Four: THE INDIVIDUALIST

    The Childhood Pattern
    Practices Which Help Fours Develop

    Keys for Reflection

Type Five: THE INVESTIGATOR

    The Childhood Pattern
    Practices Which Help Fives Develop

    Keys for Reflection

Type Six: THE LOYALIST

    The Childhood Pattern

Practices Which Help Sixes Develop

    Keys for Reflection

Type Seven: THE ENTHUSIAST

    The Childhood Pattern
    Practices Which Help Sevens Develop

    Keys for Reflection

Type Eight: THE CHALLENGER

    The Childhood Pattern
    Practices Which Help Eights Develop

    Keys for Reflection

Type Nine: THE PEACEMAKER

    The Childhood Pattern
    Practices Which Help Nines Develop

    Keys for Reflection

Conclusion

Introduction

The principles of the Enneagram have been said to be around since ancient history. Its roots can be traced back to around 4,500 years ago, in Babylon. It has also been said to have added its influence from the Jewish Kabbalah movement, Christian mysticism, and even Sufism, a mystical form of Islam. Enneagram character types were also strongly featured in Dante's *The Divine Comedy* by the mapping out of each of the characters' personal growth and transformation in the poem. George Ivanovich Gurdjieff first introduced the Enneagram methodology to his students in the 1930s. He was a spiritual teacher and introduced it as a spiritual symbol. Today, researchers focus on the psychological aspect of the Enneagram instead of the religious aspect. The Enneagram is mostly used as a self-mastery tool to develop personalities and for personal self-knowledge. Its application has also proven to be quite valuable in counseling and psychotherapy, as well as business development.

So what exactly is Enneagram? The Enneagram system describes the nine personality types and explains just how each of them interpret the world. Each of the nine personality types have a core belief system in which they operate. Their perception of the world is shaped by their personalities, and although these perceptions are not necessarily wrong, they do have their limitations. By understanding each Enneagram type, you will gain insight into behavior patterns and begin to understand how a person's core beliefs motivate them into making their decisions. This system will guide you into having a better understanding of people's reactions to stress, and to encourage personal and career development as well as deeper spiritual growth.

The Enneagram does not group people by their behavior, but by what motivates them. Each type has unique differences, and the Enneagram serves to point out each type's desires and anxieties. The Enneagram test will match you against all nine personality types and find the one that fits you the best. As you answer the questions in the Enneagram personality test, pick the answer that best describes you at the present moment and not on how you see yourself in the future. If you are not sure or not convinced that an answer accurately describes you, think back on how you were in your formative years. We tend to be more true to ourselves when we are young adults.

The Enneagram test explores the human psyche and interconnects the nine different personality types. Although we may identify with more than one personality type, the most important outcome of this test will be to show you which type you most adhere to. Once you become aware of your strengths and weaknesses, you can begin to improve your life in the most remarkable way. The nine types have been given different names based on the individual Enneagram authors. This book will use the names given by Riso and Husdon, which are:

1. The Reformer
2. The Helper
3. The Achiever
4. The Individualist
5. The Investigator
6. The Loyalist
7. The Enthusiast
8. The Challenger
9. The Peacemaker

The benefits of the Enneagram helps us to determine our own personality type without putting us in a box, while helping us see our limitations (or our box) from how we experience the world. Although our personalities allow us to express ourselves, they can limit our perspective. Challenges arise when we become stuck in our habits. By becoming aware of these patterns, our lives can become more fulfilling, our relationships can become healthier, and we can better connect to our true selves. The Enneagram will help us understand our reactions so that we can become more skillful in working with people. Our personal and work relationships will become more successful. We will learn to not take hostility and negativity personally once we understand what people are thinking and how they are feeling. We become more compassionate and tolerant of others. The Enneagram will help you identify any psychological or emotional areas that need healing. It offers personal growth and a way to develop your inner life while allowing you to experience the presence of Spirit that is within us.

The Questionnaire

The top questionnaire to follow is the Riso-Hudson QUEST, or The Quick Enneagram Sorting Test. You will be able to narrow down the possibilities for your type in less than five minutes. It will also make identification of two or three other possibilities for your type possible. The next set of questionnaires relate to the Riso-Hudson TAS (Type Attitude Sorter). There is a list of fifteen statements with a character in mind for each of the nine types. If you have not taken an Enneagram before, start with the QUEST and then the TAS to find a match. For example, say the QUEST suggests that you are a Type 6, you can go immediately to the fifteen statements on the TAS. You can check the statements associated with Type 6 and see if you score high there as well.

If it's correct, then you are on the right path. There is a possibility that a self-diagnosis could be wrong, so keep an open mind and continue to explore Type 6. If you find that the exercises have a strong effect on you, you are most likely a Type 6. Spend time reading through this book to understand your type. Meditate on the information for a while, there is no end to this discovery. Self-discovery is a continuous journey.

Once you've discovered your type, you may run through a lot of varying emotions, including contentment, embarrassment, or happiness. Once the things that you've known almost instinctively about yourself and the patterns of your life become clear, you can be certain that you have now identified your personality type.

The Riso-Hudson QUEST: The Fast Enneagram Grouping Test.
INSTRUCTIONS:
In order for the QUEST to generate the correct results, you must read and follow these easy instructions.

1. Select a paragraph, one from each of the two groups, that best describes your general behavior and attitudes that have been prevalent throughout your life.
2. Although not every phrase or description in these paragraphs may be true for you, if you agree to it being at

least 90% correct, choose it over the other two. Look at the full picture, and don't reject a paragraph just because you don't agree with some of the wording. You must agree with the overall tone of the paragraph.
3. Go with your gut, and don't over analyze the paragraphs. Your intuition will tell you which one is the right one for you. The paragraph as a whole is far more important than the individual words.

Group I (Choose A, B or C)

A. I have been independent and fairly assertive. I've always felt that it's best to meet life head on. I want to make things happen, so I set my own goals because I know exactly what I want. I don't like sitting around, I want to get involved. I work hard and I play hard; I want to achieve something big, and have an impact on this world. I'm not confrontational, but I won't let anybody push me around.

B. I tend to be quiet, and like to be on my own. I'm not much of an attention-seeker, and keep to myself in social settings. I'm not generally assertive or forceful. I'm not competitive, and don't like to take the lead on anything. I have been called a dreamer, although most of my energy goes into my imagination. I am content without being active all the time.

C. I have been extremely dedicated and responsible for most of my life. I feel guilty when I'm unable to keep my appointments and/or meet expectations. Although they don't know it, I've made personal sacrifices for many people. I've made myself available to people and I believe that I know what's best for them, and will do whatever it takes. I generally do what I want; I take just enough care of myself, if there's time. I do what needs to be done, and then I relax.

Group II (Choose 1, 2 or 3)
1. I have a positive outlook on life and believe that everything will work out in the end. I can always find something to occupy myself with and will do it with the greatest amount of enthusiasm. I enjoy being in other people's company and making them happy. There are times when I don't feel too good, but I tend to hide it from others. Staying positive for others has sometimes meant that I don't deal with my problems quickly and effectively.
2. I have such strong feelings about things that most people can tell whenever I'm not happy with something. I put my guard up when I'm around people because I'm quite a sensitive person. I make it quite clear where others stand with me, so in turn I expect to know where I stand with them. When I am worked up or upset about something, others need to respond in the same way. Although I know what needs to be done, I don't like people constantly telling me what I should do. I want to make decisions for myself.
3. I am extremely uncomfortable when dealing with feelings because I am logical and self-controlled. I am a perfectionist, and prefer to work on my own. My feelings are not brought into conflicts or problems. I've been called cool and detached because I don't show my emotions or allow them to get to me. They will only get in my way and distract me from what is really important.

Your two-digit code will be a letter from group I and a number from group II. If you find it difficult to pick one letter and one number, you may have a mix of both personalities. Keep both codes in mind and do some research on each of them. For example, if you pick B from group one, but find that 1 and 3 fits you from group II, your combination will be B1 and B3.

Interpreting THE QUEST

Join the letter and the number that you picked from the 2 digit code. If you picked paragraph C in group I, and paragraph 2 in group II, this will then produce the two letter code C2. To figure out which basic personality type the QUEST indicates that you are, look at the QUEST codes on the right (Kilson, 2020).

2 Digit Code	Type	Type Name and Key Characteristics
A1	7	The Enthusiast: Encouraging, Achieved, Impetuous
A2	8	The Challenger: Self-confident, Resolute, Domineering
A3	3	The Achiever: Flexible, Bold, Image-conscious
B1	9	The Peacemaker: Sensitive, Comforting, Over-confident
B2	4	The Individualist: Instinctive, Visual, Self-absorbed
B3	5	The Investigator: Perceptive, Advanced, Isolated
C1	2	The Helper: Nurturing, Ample, Dominant
C2	6	The Loyalist: Appealing, Accountable, Protective
C3	1	The Reformer: Logical, Principled, Self-controlled

Type One: THE REFORMER

Rather than becoming embarrassed by their flaws, Type Ones, or the Reformers, embrace their imperfections as perfections.

This personality type is known for being responsible, and are considered to be perfectionists. They take life far too seriously, and show a strong dislike towards those who don't. They are hard workers, ambitious, and driven towards perfection. Although they put great effort into making the world better, they tend to see the world in black and white. The perfectionist in them makes them appear to be critical and condescending, but their desire is to bring order and to improve on what they perceive to be chaos. Their practical nature and eye for detail make them excellent at managing, though they usually take on more than they should.

They tend to see flaws in themselves and in the people around them, as well as the situations they find themselves in. Their drive to correct these imperfections makes them so tense that they can barely relax. They act without thinking, usually because they have a strong belief in their convictions. They are difficult people to live with, and to get along with because of their high principles and uncompromising outlook. They expect everyone to follow the rules just like they do, therefore the Reformers are least likely to be spontaneous. They make excellent leaders, and have numerous interests. They are practical, hardworking and natural born organizers who are honest and reliable.

They are uncomfortable showing any kind of emotion as they see this as a sign of weakness. They may repress their anger to a point that it manifests as annoyance, frustration and fits of temper. They have a basic desire to be integrous, good and balanced. Their basic fears are being or becoming corrupt, or defective.

The Reformer's strengths include:
- Honesty
- Reliability
- Attention to detail
- Caring for the community

- Having personal values and the rights of others cause motivation
- Optimism and Idealism
- Easygoingness

The Reformer's weaknesses include:
- Perfectionism
- Being overly critical and self-righteous
- Being set in their ways
- Acting resentful
- A tendency to sermonize
- Being strongly focused on the minute details
- Being stubborn

The Childhood Pattern

As children, those who exhibit the Reformer personality type would have probably felt criticized, or more often, not good enough. There may have been many inconsistencies in their households. Condemnation or the abusive nature of their homes made them their own judges and caused them to disconnect from a parent who should have been their protector. To cope with this disconnection, they developed an obsession with avoiding mistakes and working extra hard to please and to gain acceptance. They self-policed as children, punishing themselves before anyone else could. Their own feelings were repressed because they had to toe the line and be responsible. There were never any outbursts of anger; this emotion usually showed up as clenched teeth while doing a chore. In order to outdo any expectation from them, they follow their own set of rules and code of conduct. The reformer type's psychological defense is to avoid anger and maintain an image of always being right.

Practices Which Help Ones Develop

Take time for yourself and relax. You don't have to be in control of everything, because thankfully, the world does not depend on you (although you may feel that it does). You may be an excellent teacher; however, not many people are as self-disciplined as you, so don't expect them to change right away. Self-criticism and irritation do nothing to improve yourself or anyone else, so try not to work yourself up over someone else's mistakes. Your super ego does not help you, it undermines you. Your self righteous anger alienates people whenever you become offended, just because they haven't done the right thing according to your definition of it.

Get in touch with your emotions and unconscious impulses. Try group therapy, or any kind of group work that will help you develop your emotions in a positive way. Suppressed anger and resentment can overshadow your life, especially if this is associated with what you believe to be true. Notice how others react to you when you are not judgmental or quick to point out their mistakes. The need to be right or to be in control all the time could lead to physical tension in the neck and shoulders, and sometimes even the jaw.

Be patient, don't expect others to automatically change and think the way you do. Set aside some time to relax, and delegate some tasks to others. Understand your emotions, and be in tune with them.

Keys for Reflection

Stop for a few minutes at least three times a day to center yourself and to reflect on the following:

Whenever your mind sees something as wrong that needs to be corrected, stop and notice how your mind goes into error. Discern whether it really does need to be corrected.

Whenever your inner voice becomes critical, stop and notice the amount of energy that goes into being judgmental. Practice releasing the energy from your body.

Whenever you find yourself judging others or yourself being judged, stop and notice how often you react to these feelings.

Recognize and release any and all judgements from yourself that are no longer valid.

Be kind to yourself, and be receptive to the calm and untroubled serenity that is present. Have some fun with loved ones, and develop the child within you. Revisit childhood activities that made you really happy. Set aside a portion of your day when you can just relax and reflect. Alternately, take scheduled breaks during the course of your workday to avoid burning out. Uplift your mood with laughter.

Type Two: THE HELPER

Unlike Type-Ones, Type-Two personality types (or the Helpers) like to focus on caring for others, rather than themselves.

This personality type is made up of selfless, caring individuals who are always ready to jump in and assist others. They tend to focus on building relationships, and are excellent at making friends. They are supportive and generous, and they're so invested in people that they remember everyone's birthdays. They are truly interested in what they perceive as the good things in life, such as family, love and friendship. They are constantly looking for opportunities to make a difference. People are drawn to the Helper personality type because of their warm hearts, and the appreciation and attention that they're given.

The love and affection that this personality type gives does have another side, though. Their need for appreciation can make them overextend themselves to gain affection from others, and they often end up with a sense of entitlement. They become bossy, intrusive, and manipulative, and feel justified in doing so. They are emotional sponges; they find it difficult to set boundaries or get angry. Putting others first does eventually make the Helper personality type secretly resentful, and although they work really hard to repress this emotion they do erupt occasionally. They are likely to adapt themselves to earn the approval of friends and loved ones. They repress their own needs to appear helpful. They have a basic fear of being unworthy of love and a basic desire to be loved.

The Helper's strengths include:
- Communication
- Gaining popularity
- Being caring and nice
- Being sympathetic
- Being humble
- Being intuitive

The Helpers weaknesses include:
- Being naive

- Being proud and privileged
- Having poor self esteem
- Believing themselves to be indispensable
- Inflated self-importance

The Childhood Pattern

As children, those who exhibit the Helper personality felt as though they were loved only when they were helping others. They felt that there was no guidance or structure in their homes, and the only way to earn love was to repress their own needs. Even though the love they gave wasn't always reciprocated, they closed off their own needs because it felt selfish. Their security and sense of belonging comes from being needed, and their love ultimately becomes conditional. This could manifest in doing chores or taking on adult responsibilities as a way to earn the love others take for granted. Love was defined by giving and not receiving.

Practices Which Help Twos Develop

First, address your own needs, as it will ensure that you are able to meet anyone else's without resentment and frustrations. It's common sense to make sure that you have taken care of yourself before seeing to the needs of others. Before you decide to assist someone, think about what your motives are for doing so. Do you expect something in return? If you do, you may be setting yourself up for a bitter disappointment. Although it is an admirable trait to be there for someone, it's always good to ask what it is that they really need. Just because you have an intuitive feeling of their needs does not mean that they want you to meet those needs. Communication is key, and if they decline your offer to help, accept their decision gracefully. Be careful to not remind anyone of what you've done for them, allow them to thank you in their own way. They are by no means rejecting you if they don't give you the recognition you desire or if they decline your offer to help.

These personality types experience tension around their chest and diaphragm areas. The energy build up in their upper bodies makes it difficult to stay grounded and they become dramatic and talkative. They usually turn their repressed feelings into physical symptoms.

Recognize that your own needs are just as important as the needs of others. You will not be able to meet the needs of others if your own needs are not met. Although sometimes it's good to jump in and assist, you do need to take a break sometimes.

Keys for Reflection

Without judging yourself, take note of reasons why you help and heal those around you. What is it that fuels your need to be indispensable? There is absolutely no need for you to repress your own desires by fulfilling the needs of others. You are valued and loved for who you are, and not for what you do for others. Take back your giving energy, and know with great confidence that it is just as important to receive. Take deep, slow breaths, and nurture and love yourself with each breath you take. Take note of how others respond to you as you care for yourself. Open up your heart to experience what you truly desire for yourself.

Explore your artistic side with art or music therapy, and unleash your feelings. Go shopping, change your style, or create a unique look for yourself.

Spend time learning who you truly are, and take a journey into discovering yourself. Investigate your heritage and family tree.

Spend some time on your own to heal, invest in yourself, and become a stronger version of yourself. Develop yourself spiritually and emotionally.

Type Three: THE ACHIEVER

Type-Three personalities, or the Achievers, are focused on becoming the best, most real versions of themselves.

The Achiever personality types are hardworking and driven; they really can do anything they set their minds to. They are usually the most successful, and are often regarded as self-made. They are always looking for something to excel at, or to add to their already impressive skill set. People with this personality type are feelings-based, highly adaptable, and both set and achieve high personal and career goals. Their charismatic nature is what others find contagious, and they become role models who inspire others to do and be all that they are destined to be. Type three personalities become so consumed by their need to succeed and by their successes that they often become unconsciously afraid of failing. This unconscious fear leaves them with a sense of shame, which in turn leaves them with a fear of intimacy. They shy away from close relationships in order to keep their fears hidden. They tend to keep their focus on being productive and the rewards to go with this, which often means that they lose their true selves in the process.

Although they are likable, they are also really difficult people to get to know. They keep up the appearance of being successful and happy, while they hold an underlying fear of being a "nobody." Their success is defined by their families and their social and cultural environments, and they will always strive to be somebody in their community. To them, having status is better than having no value in the eyes of their families and communities. Type-Three personalities are generally known as people of action, and not for their feelings. They tend to subdue any emotion that gets in the way of what they're trying to achieve. They have a basic fear of being worthless, and their basic desire is to feel worthwhile and valued.

The Achiever's strengths are:
- Success
- Achievement
- Enthusiasm

- Self-motivation
- Authenticity
- Energy
- Artistic ability
- Resiliency

The Achiever's weaknesses are:
- Vanity
- Overworking themselves
- Competition
- Impatience
- Being overly image-conscious

The Childhood Pattern

As children, these types were probably not allowed to show their feelings or be themselves. They had to put on a fake persona to be accepted, and because acceptance and attention was what they desired, this behavior became a way of life for them. They learned at a very young age to recognize behavioral patterns and activities that adults valued and appreciated. They learned that they were loved for what they did and for who they were. Therefore, in order to gain their parents' praise, they learned to perform rather than be themselves. Type-Threes are straight A students who will have lots of medals and trophies. However, gradually they began to lose touch with their true self and eventually lose the desires of their own heart.

The Achievers need to let go of their social image and find their inner self. Their defense mechanism is usually to pretend to be someone other than themselves to maintain an image of looking successful. They tend to build up tension in their chest area, so they really do need to watch out for heart attacks. Because they put so much effort into productivity, they have an underlying sadness within themselves.

Practices Which Help Threes Develop

Take note of your enthusiasm in accomplishing goals. Are you seeking approval for accomplishing the tasks, or are you driven by the accolades and recognition from those around you? Become aware that the driving desire to get ahead is actually taking you away from your true emotions. Once you become aware of this, pull your energy back inside yourself and breathe. Take slow deep breaths and self-observe. Love comes from being yourself and by doing other activities. Release the pressure that comes with being impatient by slowing yourself down; by doing this, you are actually increasing your pace. Allow you own true feelings and the feelings of others into your heart. You are not dependent on your efforts; become aware of how others respond to you when you open your heart.

Acknowledge that others have potential and encourage them to grow, instead of having the spotlight focused on yourself. Apologize when you're wrong, and practice being more genuine and less pretentious.

Keys for Reflection

Stop for a few minutes each day to center yourself and to reflect on the following:

Take note of how trying to gain the approval of others by looking good can ruin your life. You don't need to behave in a certain way to be recognized; just be who you were meant to be. Allow your true emotions to enter into your heart.

Focus your attention away from performing, slow your pace down, and take notice of what you're doing. Reclaim and recall your feelings, and encourage them to manifest. Let things be as they are, as you cultivate your own feelings.

Slow down and open your heart to yourself and to others; show compassion and patience for the way things are. Be kind to yourself, and become receptive to the energy that's presenting itself to you.

Cultivate a stillness within yourself and allow things to be as they should. Exercise patience with yourself and allow your true feelings to arise. Allow your heart to open itself to others and be compassionate towards the plights of others.

Type Four: THE INDIVIDUALIST

Though each personality type is unique in its own way, Type-Four personalities (or, the Individualists) truly *believe* that they are unique.

They are identity seekers who see themselves as either a gift or a curse. They see themselves as being set apart from the common people, but this also separates them from the joys in life that others enjoy so easily. They are extremely sensitive, and often feel as though they're underappreciated. They enjoy standing out from the rest of the world with their unconventional sense of style and relentless drive to self-discovery; you can always find them at flea markets and other unique places. Individualists are always pursuing creative outlets such as art or music, they usually see themselves as having a one-of-a-kind talent and their goal is to ultimately present this to the world. Because they see themselves as unique, they think that no one understands them or will be able to love them enough. They take the way they present themselves very seriously, and are therefore constantly trying to align their values to every decision they make. These Individualists own their feelings, and although they may not like what they see, they don't deny or hide them. They are willing to understand the truth, and will most probably share personal and shameful aspects about themselves.

They do have a tendency to withhold themselves whenever they feel vulnerable, and can become moody or temperamental. Their melancholic nature and low self-esteem can send them into bouts of depression. One of the challenges they face is letting go of their past hurts and experiences. They have an open heart, although they entwine both their joys and their suffering. One of their defenses is to bring outside values and present them to others to project an authentic self-image.

Their basic fear involves having no personal significance, and their basic desire is to create an identity for themselves. They have a tendency to withdraw and become depressed, or they spill out their feelings and keep close contact with others. They express themselves through creative works such as music, writing, dancing or anything else that can get their emotions balanced. The type four personalities tend to collect their energy in the midsection of their bodies, and this can lead them to become withdrawn.

The Individualist's strengths include:
- Compassion
- Idealism
- Emotional depth
- Open Heartedness
- Warmth
- Welcoming demeanor
- Artistic ability

The Individualist's weaknesses include:
- Moodiness
- Uncooperativeness
- Withdrawnness
- Envy
- Melancholy
- Dissatisfaction
- Acting detached

The Childhood Pattern

As children, those who exhibit Type-Four behavior have more than likely felt a disconnect between themselves and their parents. Their reasons for feeling cut off or abandoned could not be understood. They were often either abused when they were younger, or felt as though their parents were distant. The advice they received was generic, and not tailored to what the individualist needed. They developed a coping mechanism to deal with the rejection and isolation they felt.

Practices Which Help Fours Develop

Open your heart, and in judging yourself, take notice of your longing for fulfillment and the ideals you desire. The emotions you feel come from a sense of inner loss. Gather all the energy that you have invested into this emotion, and bring it down. Breathing into your center allows your feelings to come and go with each heartbeat. Be grateful for the here and now, and don't focus on what you think is missing. Remind yourself of the love you have irrespective of how you perceive yourself to be. Become aware of how others respond to you when you appreciate yourself.

Embrace all the positive emotions that are out there. Acknowledge that you have many of the good qualities that you admire in others. Build your identity around your uniqueness, your gifts, and your talents.

Keys for Reflection

Stop for a few minutes each day to reflect on the following:

Take note of how your energy and attention returns to what you feel is missing in your life. Allow yourself to be present and positive, to observe the intensity of your feelings, and to come back to a calm and sense of peace.

Turn the ordinary into the extraordinary by noticing how often your focus is on being different and not on the ordinary. Be grateful in the present; acknowledge that nothing of value is missing.

Be kind and appreciate yourself, and treat others as your equals. Get rid of envy by cultivating happiness with others around you. Have a generous heart, and be confident that nothing is actually missing.

Type Five: THE INVESTIGATOR

Type-Fives, or Investigators, are among the more introspective personality types. They like to focus on finding a balance between their feelings of isolation and their feelings of belonging.

This personality type is curious, innovative and independent. They become so preoccupied with developing ideas and skills that they can become detached and intense. They are called the Investigator because it so aptly describes this personality type. They want to know everything–how the world works, and why it operates in the ways that it does. They are continually searching and questioning, and very rarely except the answers they're given. They want to test it out for themselves. They observe and contemplate, they are listening and/or taking notes, even if it is just on an anthill in the backyard. They become extremely self-confident in the knowledge that they've gained. They love to gather information and process it into new ideas. Because their identities are built around being someone who has ideas or has something new and insightful to share, knowledge and understanding are highly valued by them. It is for this reason Type-Five personalities are drawn to the unusual, the secrets of the universe, the bizarre, and the unthinkable. By investigating the unknown, they believe that this is a way of gaining independence. Type-Five personalities are generally scholars or technical experts. They are perceptive and analytical.

These Investigators have the ability to detach themselves from others who they feel are intrusive. Although they enjoy their freedom, they can also become lonely. Even though they are intellectually brilliant, relationships prove to be the most challenging for them. They would rather escape into the safety of their mind to figure out how to cope with the world around them, because they have a deep insecurity about doing well in the real world. They have been known to cut themselves off from their friends and family, develop tunnel vision, and even lose their grip on reality. As a result, they often lose friendships in the process.

Although it may be uncomfortable, they have to find a way to balance their withdrawal from others and reaching out to them. Their basic fear is to be incapable or helpless, and their basic desire is to be competent.

They avoid feelings of loneliness and emptiness by appearing knowledgeable and self-reliant. They use physical separation to cut off their emotions. They get stuck in their heads and it takes great effort to bring them back. They become sensitive to sound and touch, and tension gathers in their middle.

The Investigator's strengths include:
- A Craving for knowledge
- Scholasticism
- Self-reliance
- Perception
- Rationality and technicality
- Trust
- Privacy
- Curiosity

The Investigator's weaknesses include:
- Isolation
- Stinginess
- Non-attachment
- Excessive intellectualism
- Withholding of information
- Absentmindedness
- Thoughtfulness
- Vulnerability

The Childhood Pattern

As children, this personality type was probably not sure where they belonged. They were likely always on the outside looking in, instead of being accepted as part of the group. It's possible that they received no interaction or affection from their adult caregivers. They might have put up walls around themselves as a defense, and retreated into their minds to block out intrusive parents. Their family lives could have been abusive, or they just felt misunderstood. They were the children that hid in their bedrooms to read or to master some subject or another. They have learned to distance themselves and ask little from people, so that they in turn avoid expectations placed on them.

Practices Which Help Fives Develop

With a warm, open-hearted approach, take note of the tendency to detach yourself from feelings. You hold yourself back with an energy you cannot do without. You believe that to protect yourself from the demands of this world, you must have time and space for yourself. Believe that you have enough energy to become completely invested into your feelings and have confidence that you will not be drained, but nourished. Breathe into your center, into your belly and connect with your feelings. Remind yourself to not pull away from others, but be aware that it's your protective mindset that is draining your energy. You are supported by others, especially when your heart is open.

Embrace the vast amount of knowledge you already have but realize that you don't need to know everything. You need people to help you get in touch with your humanity. Take their advice and listen to their opinions; this may lead you to a whole new world of discovery.

Keys for Reflection

Stop for a few minutes at least three times a day to center yourself and to reflect on the following:

Open up your heart with confidence, knowing that you will not be drained of your energy; instead, you will be nurtured.

Notice what happens in your body when you withdraw from intrusions. Let this be the signal to remind you to relax.

Tell yourself that the protective habits you have put in place are actually restricting your needs and desires. This will lead to deprivation, the opposite of nourishment.

Whenever you find yourself feeling as though your energy is being depleted, remind yourself that you need to come back to the natural flow of the universe's energy. You will know whatever you need to know, and you will accept that you will be at peace with no knowing. You have enough knowledge. Be generous with life's abundant energy, and as you breathe in the flow of natural energy, understand that you will receive what you need.

Type Six: THE LOYALIST

Type-Sixes, or Loyalists, truly live up to their name – though they often need to face their fears to find their communities.

These personalities are excellent troubleshooters; they are committed, hardworking and responsible. They have the uncanny ability to foresee problems. They are one the most loyal people to have around. They will literally "go down with the ship" and hang on to their friends and families much longer than others would. They find their fit in the world on a social level and will be dedicated to those relationships as a result. Trust is of great importance to a Loyalist, and they find comfort in knowing that others have their backs. They need the security and commitment of their group of peers, and they will stand those who they view as strong. Inner peace is a challenge for many, but with time and effort, they are able to reach their goals of trust and confidence. They are very thoughtful, and will move their colleagues forward in front of themselves. As team players, they take pride in serving others and will make an extra effort to develop skills that will benefit their organization. Although they can be quite skeptical, they are also mentally astute; they are fully aware of their shortcomings, and their self-esteem may even fluctuate.

Whenever Type-Six personalities over analyze information, they feel anxious and become restless, imagining the worst possible scenario. This usually makes them paranoid, and they then become deluded into thinking that they're in constant danger. Not all Type-Six personalities are easygoing, some of them can be quite rebellious to a point of being revolutionary. They end up fighting for their beliefs far more vehemently than for themselves. They will become competitive, and in some cases, arrogant. Their basic fear is not having the support and guidance they need and their basic desire is to have strong support and security.

Type-Six personalities often hesitate and worry. They brace themselves for risks, and as a result, Myopia is common because their eyes become suspicious, guarded, fearful and even protruding.

Their diaphragm holds quite a bit of tension, which sometimes produces a halting way of speech.

The Loyalist's strengths include:
- Strategic thinking
- Loyalty
- Courage
- Attentiveness
- Organization
- Being a team player
- Commitment
- Authenticity

The Loyalist's weaknesses are:
- Suspiciousness
- Pessimism
- Playing devil's advocate
- Doubtfulness
- Unnecessary self-limitation
- Pushiness or unnecessary aggression
- Stubbornness, or inability to forgive
- Skepticism

The Childhood Pattern

As children, Type-Six personalities may have been raised in unsafe and/or unpredictable circumstances. Although they did have a connection to the adult figures in their lives, it wasn't always a positive connection. They learned to depend on themselves for guidance as a result. They developed a tendency to internalize their anger, which often led to some kind of self-destruction. They became distrustful, and would rebel if they felt that an authoritative figure lost their trust. Although they crave the assurance of supportive friends and family, they have a lot of distrust in them as well.

Practices Which Help Sixes Develop

Without being judgmental towards yourself, take note of how your concerns of perceived hazards fuel your energy into underlying fears and doubt. Remind yourself that you don't have to be questioning everything in order to set your mind at ease. Believe that you are loved, secure, and valued, and that the world is not as hazardous as you think it is. Take whatever energy is in your mind and direct that energy into the center of your belly, calming your mind. You don't need to face challenges by thinking negatively. Take note of the positives in your life, and put your energy on them. Notice how others respond to you when you have faith in yourself.

No one is exempt from anxiety, so whatever you're experiencing is not unique to you. Take control of your fears and learn to manage your reactions. Give others the benefit of doubt and take a chance on building lasting relationships.

Keys for Reflection

Stop for a few minutes at least three times a day to center yourself and reflect on the following:

When you feel fear entering into your body, find out whether there is a real threat or just a challenge. Most of the time you are just magnifying something that has the appearance of fear.

Remember, you have a blindspot when it comes to fear. Your imagination is making what you're experiencing feel a hundred times worse than it actually is. Move to remedy this, instead of moving away from it.

Release any doubts or contrary thoughts whenever they creep into your mind. This is the only way you will be able to move forward.

Be kind and open-hearted to yourself and practice a few times a day. It only takes a minute or two out of your day to receive the energy and obtain natural courage. Move toward, and not against, any fearful situation you may find yourself in. Be observant, and discern what is real and what isn't real. Have faith in yourself and in life, to directly towards fearful situations and make fear your friend. Cultivate courage, not worst-case scenarios.

Type Seven: THE ENTHUSIAST

Type-Sevens, or the Enthusiasts, are adventurers at heart. They embrace their feelings as they would their next adventure.

This personality type are playful, versatile extroverts. They are high-spirited, and they are enthusiastic in just about everything. They pursue whatever they want in life, they are determined, and they love a sense of adventure. They can also be a bit scatterbrained and undisciplined. They are quick learners, and have the ability to absorb languages, procedures, etc. They are also forward-thinkers and movers, they have an interest in a wider variety of things. They like to keep their options open, and don't like limitations. They don't care about other people's opinions of themselves, they just want to have some fun. They have endless energy and relentless curiosity. The Enthusiasts are like kids in a candy store, and treat the world as their playground. They are highly productive and charismatic and will face any challenge head on. They find the lessons in every experience whether it is good or bad, and they're constantly seeking the next high.

Although they are able to learn many different things with ease, it makes it difficult to pick one to focus on. They become distracted so easily that many of them find it difficult to stay on course. Type-Seven personalities are not too good at focusing, because they always believe that something bigger and better is waiting for them. As a result of this they don't place value in their abilities. They can be self-centered and downplay their faults; they are often reluctant to acknowledge their negative emotions. They are susceptible to depression and anxiety disorders. For fear of missing out, Type-Sevens will cram as much activity into their lives as possible while their real desires are hidden deep inside them.

They burn out quickly, become overly critical, and get annoyed at the little details. Type-Seven personalities' energy moves out of their bodies and therefore, they remain over-stimulated at most times. Instead of facing physical pain, they struggle to stay grounded and any pain that they experience is explained away. They have a basic fear of being in pain, or of being deprived. Their basic desire is to fulfill their needs and to be content.

The Enthusiast's strengths include:
- Adventurousness
- Quick thinking
- Positive Attitude
- Popularity
- Fun-lovingness
- Optimism
- Light-heartedness

The Enthusiast's weaknesses include:
- Self-absorption
- Lack of commitment
- Over consumption of ideas or experiences
- Fear of missing out
- Opinionation
- Hard-headedness

The Childhood Pattern

As children, they may have felt disconnected from, or been removed from nurturing too early. They may have found that they couldn't count on anyone other than themselves. The nurturer could have been any family member that was responsible for them. Whatever the reason for this, miscommunication or abuse, Type-Seven personalities focused on transitional activities to fill the gap to nurture themselves, because they couldn't rely on others to fill the emptiness. They found distractions to fulfill their needs, and to repress all their fears. Everything that brought them even a little bit of happiness became a symbol of nurturing.

Practices Which Help Sevens Develop

Open your heart and ground yourself, and without judgments, take note of how your mind races through the different plans and possibilities that are driven by your energy. This comes from your belief that in order to feel loved and secure, you must undertake all of life's adventures. You will be able to see how by escaping you've been limiting yourself, and thus robbing yourself of a holistic life. Breathe into the center of gravity in your belly and bring down your energy. Concentrate on the flow of your breathing, and accept all the feelings that come to the fore. Focus on accepting both the joys and the sorrows that life brings. Take note of how others respond to you when you accept that life has to offer you.

Create more opportunities for yourself by listening to the ideas of others. Weigh the positives and negatives of any choice or decision before embarking on them. This will add great value and benefit to you in the long term.

Keys for Reflection

Stop for a few minutes at least three times a day to center yourself, and to reflect on the following:

Whenever you plan for positive outcomes, notice that your energy levels fluctuate. Bring yourself back to the full present of the moment and allow yourself to see both the pain and the joy.

Notice that your thoughts often to the things that bring you fulfillment. Now put equal amounts of energy onto others, and onto yourself.

When you sense something painful or distressing within your body, your natural response is to turn them into something positive. Breathe down to your center and face these feelings with discernment.

Show yourself kindness by practicing the following a few minutes each day. Receive the energy and be present in each moment. Focus your attention doing what's in front of you; do just one thing at a time. Practice breathing by counting each breath, start over if you lose count, keep bringing yourself into the present moment. Listen when others are talking; don't respond, just listen.

Reflect on all the emotions you may find difficult, such as sorrow and suffering.

Type Eight: THE CHALLENGER

Type-Eights, or the Challengers, must remember to let go to find love in their lives – something that can be difficult for them sometimes.

The Type-Eight personality types are strong and assertive, but also tend to be a bit egocentric. They enjoy taking on new challenges as well as giving others the opportunity to challenge them too. Their charismatic nature sees many people join them in various endeavors, from waging war to rebuilding a city. They tend to take charge and lead, which can be intimidating to others. They like to be in control, and to do things their own way. They are very protective of their friends and family. They are resourceful and honorable; they are natural-born leaders. They look after the needs of others, and ensure that the world is a better place for all. They can be fair and just, but at the same time, they can be confrontational and lose their tempers. They need to be independent, and will very rarely work for someone else. They don't see themselves in any other position but the top position. Although they may be aware of what others think of them, Type-Eight personalities don't let it bother them. They have the uncanny ability to turn lemons into the best-tasting lemonade on offer.

Although they are tough and can take any amount of physical punishment, one of their greatest fears is physical harm. This a blessing and a curse, because they overlook the health of others and their own stamina for granted. Beneath the tough exterior they present, they are quite vulnerable. They refuse to be controlled, and will not tolerate anyone having power over them. They desire to dominate their environment to prove that they are strong. These personality types are afraid of rejection, so instead of talking about it they distance themselves, so their modus operandi is to reject others first. They may then eventually shut themselves off from others, and become crude and arrogant. Their basic fear is of being controlled or harmed by others, and their basic desire is to protect themselves and be in charge of their own destinies. Their defense mechanism is to deny their feelings to maintain an image of strength. The Type-Eight personality has a huge amount of bioenergetic charge in their bodies, which attracts them to intensity.

The Challenger's strengths include:
- Generosity
- Power
- Enthusiasm
- Assertiveness
- Leadership
- Innocence
- Energy
- Supportiveness

The Challenger's weaknesses include:
- Anger
- Domineerance
- Bossiness
- Excession
- Vulnerability
- Vengeance
- Aggression
- Combativity
- Distrust

The Childhood Pattern

As children, Type-Eight personalities may have matured far too soon, and had to hide their vulnerability to appear strong. They perhaps learned to find their place in the family by taking on strong nurturing roles. If they showed any softness, they may have been rejected or hurt. They are adventurous and assertive, which often gets them punished. Because of the frequent punishments, they take on a don't-care attitude and a steely resolve. The more rejection they felt, the more hard and aggressive their response would be.

Practices Which Help Eights Develop

Without judging yourself, open up your heart to notice the urge you have to act on whatever injustices happened to you. This comes from the belief that for you to be loved and secure, you must be resolute and strong so that those with more power will not be able to take advantage of you. As the energy rises up in you, take a breath and resist the urge to take immediate action. Based solely on your version of what the truth is, can you notice the urge to act? Collect this energy and keep it in the gravitational center of your belly. What you regard as protection from being vulnerable is actually the strength of the impact. Take notice of how others react and respond to you when you allow yourself to be receptive to their truths.

Remember that people and relationships are far more important than power. Learn to make sacrifices and work alongside others. Transfer your energy to empower, uplift and inspire people.

Keys for Reflection

Take time to stop for a few minutes each day to center yourself and to reflect on the following:

Take note of the urge to act where it lives in your body. Pause and receive the gift of time, and then take relevant action. Witness the impact you have on others when you stop and breathe. Moderate your energy to fit the situation.

Remind yourself that any vulnerability you feel has a softness to accompany it, and that this is a force of great strength to compliment your energy.

Be kind to yourself and open up your heart to having an innocent mindset. Be content in the moment, and experience the power of not taking or placing blame. Embody compassion, and receive the truth in all things.

Type Nine: THE PEACEMAKER

Type-Nines, or Peacemakers, often become important participants in the conversations they engage in, as they are known for being stable and accepting.

They are creative and supportive; they want everyone to get along. They are on a quest to find peace for everyone around them. They are regarded as spiritual seekers, and thus seek out connections with the universe. They can be complacent, and will minimize problems to ensure that everything runs smoothly. The Type-Nine personality mostly draws from the psychological and spiritual worlds. Ironically, they are also grounded in the physical world, which means that they are also in touch with their instinct. The Type-Nine personality is the most basic personality of all; they are considered to be "salt of the earth" people. They have a problem with focusing on their own priorities or changing direction to something that needs attention. Although they find it difficult to make decisions for themselves, they excel as mediators. Even though they appear to be even-tempered and easygoing, they internalize their emotions.

Peacemakers can also be incredibly stubborn, and will retreat into themselves. Their response to pain is to numb it out. They also appear to live in a constant state of either spiritual enlightenment or denial, all because they want to live in peace. The nine type personalities are called "the crown of the Enneagram" because they reside at the top and seem to encompass all personalities. They are as strong as the eights, fun-loving and adventurous as the sevens, as dutiful as the sixes, as intellectual as the fives, as creative as the fours, as attractive as the threes, as generous as the twos, and as idealistic as the ones. However, they don't often have strong identities for themselves. Their basic fear is of separation and loss, and their basic desire is to have peace of mind.

In an attempt to create harmony, they resist anything that would upset them. They also avoid conflict to maintain a self-image of being harmonious. They like to stay under-charged; they're good at belly-breathing so they avoid breathing into their chest. Because they can merge so easily with others, they have difficulty setting boundaries. Their lower back is a vulnerable area.

The Peacemaker's strengths include:
- Balance
- Harmony
- Acceptance
- Acting welcoming
- Inclusivity
- Genuinity
- Adaption

The Peacemaker's weaknesses include:
- Conflict
- Stubbornness
- Lack of attention
- Ambivalence
- Taking the right course of action
- Passive aggression
- Distraction
- Aloofness

The Childhood Pattern

As children, the Type-Nine personalities were probably overlooked and felt lost as a result. They would have had to keep a low profile and tune out the problems. This was the child who put on headphones and played outside while family members fought. They learned to distract themselves from their own feelings and concentrate making others feel better. They can let go and give a voice to their anger, they can participate in the world again.

Practices Which Help Nines Develop

Open up your heart while you remain grounded, and take note of how your energy is pulled in many directions. So many environments have claimed your energy that there's none left for you. This comes from your belief that for you to be loved, you must blend in and stay in the background. Stop for a minute and breath, focus on yourself. What are your priorities and desires? What's important to you? From the gravitational center in your belly, bring your attention inside yourself and connect with it. Now set your own boundaries, limits and priorities. Love yourself as you love others. Take note of the effect you have on others when you can love yourself, and notice how everyone else responds to you when you speak up for yourself.

Set goals for yourself and tackle them one at a time. Encourage yourself with your own words of wisdom and good advice. Adapt to the changes that come; you have great potential, and you are stronger than you think.

Keys for Reflection

Stop for a few minutes at least three times a day to center yourself and to reflect on the following:

Notice how your attention automatically goes to others that need it. Use this as a marker to bring back your focus and attention to your own needs.

Take note of where the resistance is in your body, and realize that this is important to you. Explore the nature of its importance.

Whenever you get upset by conflict, feel where your body is and what it is sensing. Conflict is natural, and you must learn to deal with it constructively.

Be kind to yourself, and practice these steps each day, reminding yourself that you are equal to all others. Pick out what is of importance when you face discomfort or conflict. Discover and become aware of your intentions and purposes. Value yourself as you value others and remember what your priorities are. And whenever you feel resistance, it means that something important is inside.

Conclusion

Personality is what we see ourselves as, or what we determine to be the character traits of others. Every little thing that you do sends out information about your personality, from the reason you react in a certain way, or what you like or don't like. Our minds use this information to draw distinctions between each person we meet. Perhaps it may be possible for there to be one person who can communicate with people of all personality styles; you can be this person by reflecting on how other people behave and by doing some restructuring on your own personality. A person with a great personality will bring positivity to any situation, whereas a person who has the complete opposite personality will appear dreary and bleak. Psychologists have determined that people with unhealthy personalities have a fear disorder. This fear prevents them from opening up to others and ultimately stagnate their growth.

Although we may look quite different on the outside, we all have the same anxieties and needs. In fact we are all searching for the same things, things such as understanding and recognition. Once you have the ability to understand what motivates an individual, you will be able to interact and associate with others effectively. The Enneagram system can be used to explain almost anything in the universe, and its importance lies in the fact that it is a valuable tool to be used to improve relationships.

Here is a brief summary of each personality type, according to the Enneagram personality test.

1. The Reformers - these personality types have extremely high ideals of being the perfect person. They have a tendency to take things seriously, and will become tense if they cannot complete their work perfectly and on time. They can be sensitive to being criticized by others.
2. The Helpers - these personality types are caring, loving types, and they are always ready to be of assistance to friends and family. Although they are warm, generous and nurturing individuals, their confidence is dependent solely

on others. They cannot say no to anyone and tend to overdo things for others and don't have enough energy for themselves. They drain themselves for others and become upset if they don't get help in return.
3. The Achievers - these personality types are born to be successful. Their traits include confidence, efficiency, perseverance, friendliness, the list goes on and on. They are always comparing themselves to others who they feel perform better than them.
4. The Individualists - these personality types are warm and expressive. They enjoy the good things in life and try hard to be unique. They feel things deeply and understand the true meaning of life. They expect a lot from life and are good at forming relationships with those who understand them. They are prone to bouts of depression and stubbornness, and sometimes even jealousy. They get hurt easily, especially when they're misunderstood, because they depend on others for emotional support.
5. The Investigators - these personality types tend to be aloof and are loners. They are observers and try to analyze the world around them. Although they are kind and self-sufficient during hard times, they are not good at showing their emotions. They have a tendency to become suspicious, contentious, and even negative at times.
6. The Loyalists - these personality types are hard-working, responsible people. They are confident intellectuals who exude a warm attitude towards others. They can be poor decision makers and constantly need the approval of others before they can do something.
7. The Enthusiasts - these personality types are fun-loving, light-hearted, and happy people. They are restless adventurers who love to travel and take risks often. They are optimistic and responsible, and encourage others to be responsible too.

8. The Challengers – these personality types are authoritative and confident. They are straight-forward, and often don't realize when their way hurts others. Even though they are supportive and generous, they are uncomfortable when faced with incompetent people. They have a hard time showing or expressing their appreciation when needed.
9. The Peacemakers – these personality types avoid conflicts at a cost to make others comfortable. They are accepting and caring people, but lack the ability to make decisions. Even though they are confident, they often become confused about what it is that they really want.

Enneagrams are practical and applicable in our daily lives, as individuals and as a community; it is a comprehensive system that uses ancient wisdom, as well as modern psychology, to help us understand others as well as ourselves.

"Understanding is love's other name. If you don't understand, you can't love." Thich Nhat Hahn.

If You Enjoyed This Book In Anyway, An Honest Review Is Always Appreciated!

www.ingramcontent.com/pod-product-compliance
Lightning Source LLC
Chambersburg PA
CBHW030303030426
42336CB00009B/507